EARLY THEMES

Weather

Ready-to-Go Activities, Games,
Literature Selections, Poetry, and Everything
You Need for a Complete Theme Unit

by Ann Flagg

SCHOLASTIC
PROFESSIONAL BOOKS

NEW YORK • TORONTO • LONDON • AUCKLAND • SYDNEY

To Jay and Dana

Edited by Joan Novelli
Cover design by Vincent Ceci and Jaime Lucero
Cover art by Jo Lynn Alcorn
Interior design by Solutions by Design, Inc.
Interior illustration by Abby Carter and James Graham Hale (pages 11, 20, 23)

ISBN 0-590-13111-7

12 11 10 9 8 7 6 5 4 3   8 9/9/01/0

Contents

About this Book

Weather! Everybody talks about it. Everybody watches it. We dress for it and change our plans because of it. Weather can make us feel cheerful—or blue. It can change in an instant but it is predictable over time. To young children, weather is a topic of great interest— and something they see every day. This book is designed to help you capitalize on your students' curiosity and use weather as a natural starting point for a year-long hands-on thematic unit that introduces key science concepts and integrates your curriculum.

Inside you'll find:

◎ suggestions for setting up and maintaining a learning center;

◎ activities for launching your unit;

◎ special science notes that give you important background information about weather;

◎ ideas and instructions for setting up "My First Weather Station," including an outdoor weather station and a classroom bulletin board for recording, organizing, and communicating weather data children collect;

◎ instructions for making simple weather equipment and lessons that teach children how to use the tools;

◎ appealing cross-curricular lessons for exploring clouds, rain, sun, snow, wind, and temperature—including activities, experiments, extensions, and literature connections;

◎ suggestions for journal entries that double as an evaluation tool (see Journal Junctures throughout book, and page 8 for a reproducible journal page);

◎ a reproducible mini-book, plus poems and a finger play;

◎ age-appropriate reproducibles;

◎ suggestions for wrapping up the unit with a weather celebration.

WHY TEACH WITH THEMES?

Themes are naturally holistic. A good theme unit takes a collection of activities and addresses all facets of child development. For example, with this weather unit, children will measure rainfall, share wind poetry, and write weather words to sharpen language and cognitive skills. They'll participate in movement and finger plays for physical development and finger-paint clouds for aesthetic development. While working together as a team to report about the weather, children will develop their social and emotional skills.

Themes integrate the foundational skills you are required to teach too, helping you maximize use of time for student learning. As students participate in weather activities, they will often be involved in science, math, and language arts simultaneously. The result? Learning is meaningful, applicable, and fun for the children and for you.

Teaching with themes also increases retention of important concepts. Themes allow children to revisit concepts over time, deepening their understanding. By focusing on fewer topics in greater depth, themes can help children avoid information overload and enjoy and appreciate learning instead.

GETTING STARTED

Introducing the Unit

You can introduce your weather unit anytime! If you decide to start up when the school year begins and continue right up to the end, here's how your unit might flow.

- ◎ Set up the weather station in the first few weeks of school and gather data as the summer fades and fall begins. (See My First Weather Station, page 9.)

- ◎ Continue by concentrating your study on days when the weather is extreme. Use the Weather Walks and Watches section to focus on sun, wind, clouds, and other weather concepts. (See page 19.) Over an extended period of time your students will be able to see many changes in weather and the impact it has on their everyday lives.

- ◎ Share science background with students (included throughout the book), using their questions as a guide. Weave related experiments and explorations into your lesson plans. (See Wondering About Weather, page 33.)

Collecting Materials

Your kitchen cupboard, recycling bin, and garage will probably yield most of the supplies that you will need for this unit. Glance through the book and make a list. You may wish to write a letter to parents, sharing information about the theme and listing materials they may be able to donate.

Grouping

Each day, a couple of children will collect weather data to share at the weather station. (See page 10.) Decide in advance how you will select the "weather teams" so that children can look forward to their special days and keep an eye on the weather. For example, record children's names on a calendar and post it.

Assessment

Before beginning the theme, prepare a folder for each child. Children can decorate the outside of their folders with weather symbols and pictures. Have children use the folders to store journal entries, creative writing, art work, and reproducible activity sheets. Remind children to date material they include in their folders. Use the folders as one of the ways you assess students' learning. Share them at parent-teacher conferences too.

SETTING UP A LEARNING CENTER

Though not required, a learning center can enhance the unit in many ways. Here are some of the things learning centers can do for you and your students:

- ◎ act as a visual focal point for a theme and encourage students' interest and participation;

- ◎ allow all students to become involved in the theme, providing opportunities to work in groups as well as independently;

- ◎ provide a stimulating work area for children who want to know more and can work independently to gather information for themselves;

◎ encourage children to assist one another in various ways, giving each student a chance to shine;

◎ provide a central location for storing and displaying theme materials and long term projects.

Here's a plan for creating a weather learning center in your classroom.

1 Set up a work space that includes a table, several chairs, and a wall space. If possible, position the table next to a bulletin board. (You'll be using the bulletin board to set up My First Weather Station. See page 9.) The children can decorate the center as they create pictures and projects.

2 Display the cloud poster included with this book on the wall space. Invite children to add their own pictures that show different types of weather. (You might want to supply old magazines and let children cut out weather pictures they find.) Together, write words on cards that describe the weather pictured and position them accordingly. Add word webs and weather graphs as the class completes them.

3 Provide assorted reading materials at the center, such as:

◎ weather graphics and maps from newspapers;

◎ children's literature (see Literature Links throughout the book for suggestions);

◎ related reading materials children bring from home.

4 Use the center as an activity hub, selecting activities that connect with current weather conditions and the lessons you are teaching. Look for Learning Center Links throughout the book to keep activities fresh and flowing.

Managing Creative Movement

Sprinkled throughout this book, you'll find activities that engage children in creative movement. Here are some tips to help keep children focused during those times.

BOUNDARIES: *Provide plenty of space but establish boundaries so the children can come together quickly for the next set of instructions.*

EYES ON ME: *Wait until you have the attention of every child. Explain that you must be able to look into everyone's eyes. Provide clear instructions while all eyes are on you. After the activity begins it is difficult to give more than a sentence of additional instruction.*

FREEZE AND LOOK: *Establish a signal word that will stop all movement and direct the attention back to you. A whistle is helpful for outside activities.*

CLOSURE: *Plan an activity to help students wind down. For example, on a wind walk (see page 24), students gather balloons they've been watching in the wind as closure to their time outside.*

Professional Resources

BOOKS

In addition to the children's literature selections suggested throughout this book, you may want to be on the lookout for these and other resources.

Fun with Science by Marcia Gabet (Teacher Created Materials, 1985). Includes a mini-unit on weather with directions for making thermometers.

Quick-and-Easy Learning Centers: Science by Lynne Kepler (Scholastic Professional Books, 1995). This collection of appealing centers includes one on weather.

Weatherwatch by Valerie Wyatt (Addison Wesley, 1990). Written for upper elementary students, this book has lots of fascinating information to share.

Weather Words and What They Mean by Gail Gibbons (Holiday House, 1990). Fun facts about weather along with easy-to-understand explanations of weather terminology.

Where Puddles Go by Michael Strauss (Heinemann, 1995). Actvities for exploring the water cycle.

OTHER

Classroom Weather Station (Lakeshore Learning Materials; 800-421-5354). This interactive write-on/wipe-off poster lets students record temperature, rainfall, and wind direction.

Science Blaster (Davidson; 800-545-7677). This CD-ROM encourages scientific thinking through games and free exploration at three levels of difficulty. The Weather Globe area features weather stations for 10 different parts of the world.

Eyedroppers, thermometers, and other science supplies: Delta Education/(800) 258-1302 and Edmund Scientific/(609) 547-8880.

Journal Page

Name_____ Date_____

Topic_____

My First Weather Station

With a few simple materials, you can turn a large bulletin board into a simple interactive weather station for your classroom. Activities here introduce children to key concepts such as temperature, precipitation, and wind. You can set up the entire display from the start or begin slowly and add new elements when you and your students are ready. However you choose to set up and use the weather station, your students will develop observation skills over time as they collect weather data and organize it in meaningful ways.

Setting Up Your Weather Station

Here's how to set up a weather station that will encourage your students to think like scientists all year!

Materials

- ◎ weather station reproducibles (see pages 16-18)
- ◎ craft paper
- ◎ blue construction paper (9-by-12 inch)
- ◎ red construction paper
- ◎ index cards
- ◎ sentence strips
- ◎ chart paper

Teaching the Lesson

Note: *Steps 1–9 describe how to create each section of the weather station. Refer to the illustration on page 11 to see how it all comes together.*

1. Cover a bulletin board with craft paper. Make and post colorful letters that read *My First Weather Station.*

2. Staple five sheets of 9-by-12-inch blue construction paper across the top of the display to represent the sky each day. Label Monday through Friday, as shown. (Laminate first for durability, if desired.)

3. Reproduce several copies of the Sky Watch Symbols (see page 16) and cut apart the symbols. Staple nine index cards to the display to make pockets to hold the sky watch symbols. Paste one symbol to the front of each pocket. Place remaining symbols inside corresponding pockets.

4. Reproduce the Daily Temperature Graph (see page 17) and post it as shown. Cut out strips of red construction paper (1/2-inch-wide). Staple an index card next to the graph to hold the strips.

5. Write Today's Weather Report on a sentence strip and post as shown. Each day you record the weather, you can display the report under this heading at the weather station.

6. Copy and display the Rain Gauge. (See page 18.) To record rainfall, make an arrow by cutting off the corner of an envelope and taping it to a large paper clip. Clip the arrow along the left side of the rain gauge picture.

7. Write Precipitation Graph on a sentence strip. Display on the bulletin board. About 12 inches below the sentence strip, place three index cards on which you've written the words *sun, rain, snow.* (Draw pictures of each to provide visual clues for early readers.) Students will use the sky watch symbols each week to create picture graphs of the weather.

8. Display a large piece of lined paper for a Weather Words chart. Add words to the list as your unit progresses.

9. When your station is ready for your young meteorologists, go to pages 12–15, where you'll find hands-on activities for introducing each part of the weather station.

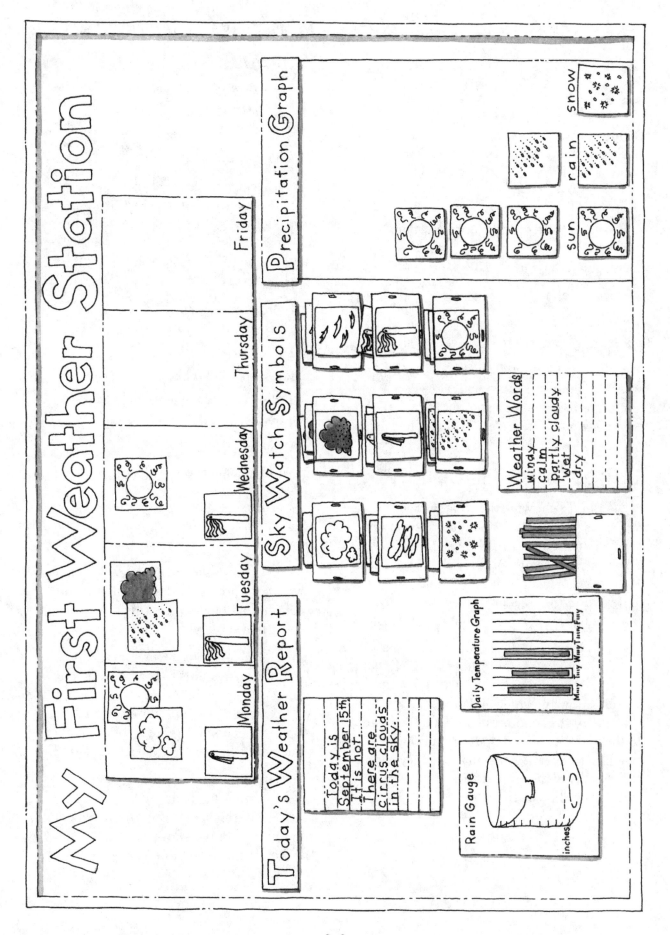

My First Weather Station

Monday   Tuesday   Wednesday   Thursday   Friday

Today's Weather Report

Today is
September 15th.
It is hot.
There are
cirrus clouds
in the sky.

Rain Gauge

inches

Daily Temperature Graph

Many Tiny Many Tiny Many Tiny Firy

Sky Watch Symbols

Weather Words
windy
calm
partly cloudy
wet
dry

Precipitation Graph

sun   rain   snow

Sky Watch

Students watch a weather forecast then use picture symbols to guide their own weather report.

Materials

- a video tape of last night's weather report
- television and VCR
- chart paper
- marker

Preparation

The evening before this lesson, tape the weather report on your local television station or arrange for a student to tape the weather report. Reserve a VCR and television for your class.

INTRODUCING THE CONCEPT

1 Before showing the weather report discuss the job of a meteorologist or read a book like *I Can Be a Weather Forecaster* by Claire Martin (Children's Press, 1987). Ask: Why do you think weather reports and weather forecasting are important to boys and girls? Farmers? Pilots? And so on.

2 Explain that the children are about to become weather forecasters. Ask them to listen carefully to the forecast for weather words. Show the video and discuss the words they heard the reporter using. Add the words to the weather words chart. Encourage children to use the vocabulary as they give their own weather reports. (See At the Weather Station, step 5.)

AT THE WEATHER STATION

Materials

- a window or door that looks outside
- sky watch symbols
- precipitation graph
- chart paper

1 Select two children each day to be weather reporters. (See Grouping, page 5.) Here's a song the class can sing each morning to introduce the daily weather report (to the tune of "Frère Jacques").

Hello weather team. (class)

Hello boys and girls. (weather team responds)

Look at the sky. (class)

Look up high! (class)

Tell us what the weather is.

Tell us what the weather is.

Won't you please?

Won't you please?

2 Have the day's weather team look outside and observe the sky as the class sings the song.

3 Next, ask the weather team to choose sky watch symbols that match the weather outside and tape them to the paper sky for that day.

4 At the end of the week, return sky watch symbols to the pockets and transfer one precipitation or sun symbol from each day to the Precipitation Graph. This graph will become a record of the number of sunny, rainy, and snowy days each month.

5 To extend this activity, have the weather team give a daily oral report. As the children speak, record the date and weather report on chart paper and display at the weather station. (See Today's Weather Report, page 11.)

Take My Temperature

Students will discover that as the temperature rises, so does the mercury in the thermometer.

Materials

◎ oral thermometers

◎ thermos containing hot water

◎ thermos containing ice water

◎ 1 plastic thermometer per group

◎ clear plastic tumblers (2 per group)

Note: *This activity introduces children to the concept of how a thermometer measures temperature. Initially, children observe the differences in temperature as the mercury moves up and down and use strips of red paper to represent the temperature. Later, children may be ready to assign numerical values to the mercury heights.*

INTRODUCING THE CONCEPT

1. Place an oral thermometer in your mouth for a few moments. Remove the thermometer and ask a volunteer to explain what you are doing. Ask: How do you use thermometers around your home? Guide the discussion to include the word *thermometer* and the concept of temperature.

2. Divide children into groups of three. Give each group a plastic thermometer and allow time to handle it and study it closely. Demonstrate how to make the mercury rise by enclosing the bulb or bottom of the thermometer in your fist.

3. Ask: How do you think the mercury would behave if you placed the thermometer in a cup of cold water? Have children stand beside their chairs and pantomime their predictions by standing up tall or crouching down low.

4. Pass out tumblers full of cold water. Have children place the thermometer in the water for two minutes to test their predictions. Have everyone stand again and pantomime what they observed.

5. Repeat the sequence for the warm water: predict, pantomime, and test.

6. To close the lesson, ask: Why do you think this information is important?

AT THE WEATHER STATION

Materials

◎ a large outdoor thermometer

◎ strips of red construction paper (1/2-inch wide)

◎ temperature graph (see page 17)

1. Place a thermometer outdoors. (You can make this a permanent placement or have students take the thermometer out each day, in which case they'll need to wait a few minutes before taking a reading.)

2. Have the children take a strip of red paper and line up the bottom of the mercury and the bottom of the red strip. Cut off the top of the strip so that it is exactly the same height as the mercury in the thermometer. Older children may also record the temperature in degrees by writing the number at the top of the red strip.

3. Back in the classroom, staple the red strip to the temperature graph. Check the temperature several times during the day. Is the temperature going up or down?

4. Repeat this at the same time each day with a new team of weather reporters. How do the daily temperatures compare?

ACTIVITY Extension Purchase a zipper that is the same length as your outdoor thermometer. Glue it to a piece of oak tag then write the degree numbers along the side. Have children zip (or unzip) the display thermometer to the corresponding temperature reading that day.

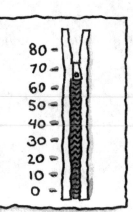

SCIENCE/MATH

Catching the Rain

Help students understand how a rain gauge works by making it rain in the classroom!

Materials

- ◎ empty 2-liter plastic bottle
- ◎ scissors or knife
- ◎ permanent marker
- ◎ a dishpan or other large tray
- ◎ a watering can
- ◎ water
- ◎ rain gauge reproducible (see page 18)

INTRODUCING THE CONCEPT

1 Build a rain gauge by cutting off the top third of the plastic bottle and inverting the top inside the bottom to form a funnel. Use a permanent marker to record inches on the side of the bottle.

2 Explain that people who report on the weather need to know how much it rains each day. Introduce your rain gauge and have children brainstorm ways the class can use the tool to learn about rainfall.

3 Demonstrate how a rain gauge works: Set the gauge in a pan and use a watering can to simulate a rainstorm over the pan. After the "storm," have a child study the rain gauge and report on the rainfall. Ask: Did all the rain fall into our rain gauge? How will the rain gauge help us gather information about the weather? Empty the gauge and vary the demonstration so that the children can report on a light rain, a heavy rain, and a day with no rain at all.

AT THE WEATHER STATION

1 Help children select an outdoor location for the rain gauge and stabilize the gauge. Look for a level spot away from buildings and trees. You can stabilize the gauge in a variety of ways: Using rocks or bricks to support the bottle is one way.

2 Each morning have the weather team visit the rain gauge then give a report at My First Weather Station. Did it rain? If so, have the team adjust the arrow to indicate the water level in the rain gauge. Remind the weather team to dump out the rain water after each reading.

Wind Friend

Use a fan to demonstrate how the wind can blow before making an actual wind observation.

Materials

- ◎ a variable-speed fan
- ◎ one set of "wind friend" symbols per child (see page 16)
- ◎ a wooden stake
- ◎ stapler
- ◎ 3 strips of lightweight, durable cloth (2 inches wide-by-half the height of the stake)
- ◎ hammer
- ◎ several small nails

INTRODUCING THE CONCEPT

1. Build a wind friend by lining up the ends of the strips of cloth and fanning them out so the strips are not laying on top of one another. Staple the strips together. Place the stapled end on top of the stake and hammer in several nails to attach the strips to the stake.

2. Explain that weather forecasters watch the wind because winds often bring changes in the weather. Then show children the wind friend. Ask: How do you think we can use this tool to learn about the wind?

3. To demonstrate the wind friend, give each child a set of wind friend symbols. (The symbols indicate the presence or absence of wind only, not direction.) Have a volunteer hold the wind friend upright in front of a fan. Turn the fan on and have children hold up the picture that best illustrates what they observe. Turn the fan off and repeat.

4. Use the reproducible wind friend pictures as models to make additional pictures representing a gentle breeze and a strong wind. Make copies for children then continue adjusting the speed of the fan and holding up cards until the children can represent wind speed with ease.

AT THE WEATHER STATION

1. Hammer the stake into the ground in an open place, preferably next to the rain gauge.

2. Each morning, have the weather team bring along the wind friend pictures as they check the rain gauge. After watching the wind friend for a few moments, have children select the picture that best shows what they observed.

3. Back in the classroom, have children place the symbol on the sky watch picture for the day and share a report on the wind conditions.

Sky Watch Symbols

Daily Temperature Graph

Monday　　**Tuesday**　　**Wednesday**　　**Thursday**　　**Friday**

Rain Gauge

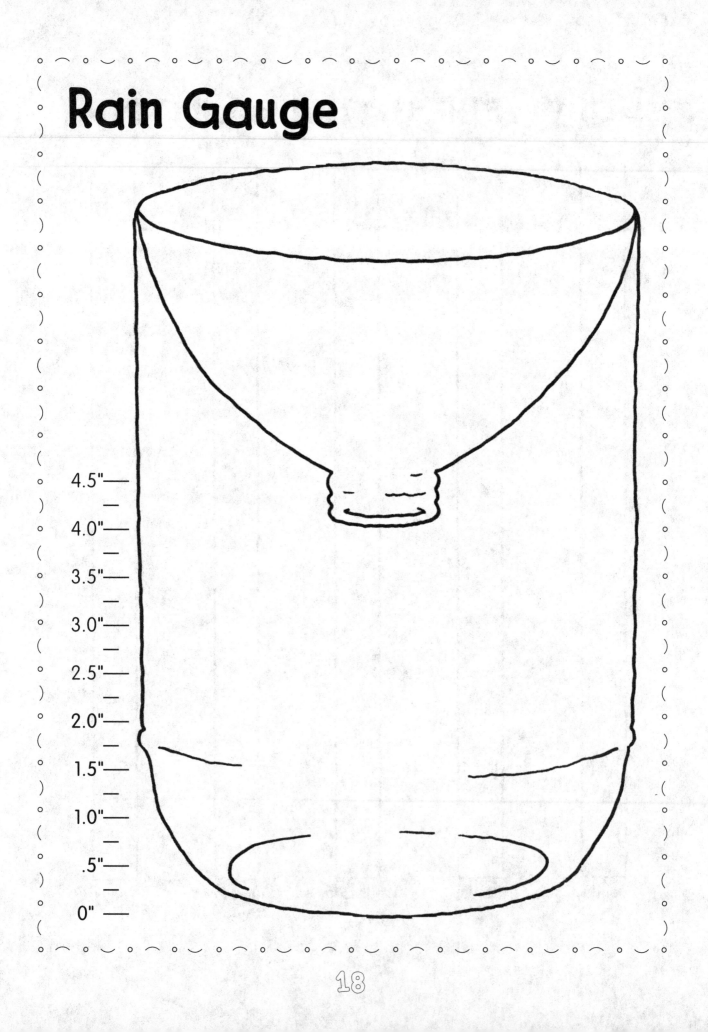

4.5"—
—
4.0"—
—
3.5"—
—
3.0"—
—
2.5"—
—
2.0"—
—
1.5"—
—
1.0"—
—
.5"—
—
0"—

Weather Walks and Watches

Clouds, wind and rain—the best way to learn about weather is to open the classroom door and take a look! In this section you'll find lessons that take advantage of days when weather is "happening." From a Fluffy Cloud Walk to a Rainy Day Walk, these mini-excursions invite children to explore their world—and begin to build connections to key science concepts. If you want to keep the activities inside, keep in mind that your students can make many meaningful observations from a window too. To deepen children's understanding—whether they're outside in the weather or watching from a window—you'll find follow-up indoor activities that explain and expand on concepts.

What Are You Wearing?

Before each weather walk, bring students together at a graph to record what they are wearing: short sleeves, long sleeves, or a jacket. Over the course of the year, children will understand that clothing changes with the weather.

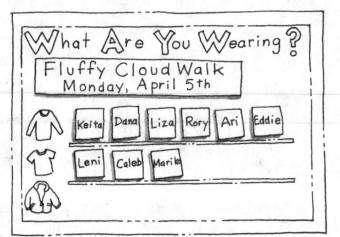

SCIENCE NOTES

During warm weather, we often wear light-colored clothing that allows air to move over our bodies. Our bodies are naturally warm. Short sleeves allow body heat to escape. This helps keep us cool. When it is cold outside, we wear long sleeves and coats. Winter clothing traps body heat and keeps cold air out. This helps keep us warm.

Materials

◎ butcher paper

◎ graph markers (one per child)

◎ sentence strips

◎ 2 index cards

Preparation

Make a graph on a piece of butcher paper to record what children wear for each walk. Show long sleeves, short sleeves, and a jacket. (See above, right.) Laminate or cover it with clear contact paper so it will last the school year. Display the graph near the learning center. Make a graph marker for each child. Markers can be simple—self-sticking notes with children's name or individual photographs, trimmed to size with Velcro on both the back of the photo and the graph.

Teaching the Lesson

1. Gather everyone around the graph. Tape a sentence strip that identifies the weather walk (for example, Fluffy Cloud Walk) and the date on the top of the graph. Help the class to understand how the graph is organized.

2. Have children place markers in the appropriate column to show what they are wearing for the walk. How many children are wearing short sleeves? Long sleeves? Jackets? Why?

3. Leave up the graph. Periodically—for example, when you're taking a new weather walk—ask children to recall what they wore on the previous walk and compare what they are wearing outside on that day.

ACTIVITY Extension When children are outside, get into the habit of saying: Guess what the temperature is today? Accept several estimates and then check the actual temperature. (Or, if the thermometer is not set up outside, tell children the temperature.) At first, their estimates may be way off, but temperature sense will improve throughout the year.

Learning Center Link

Display a stuffed teddy bear and a collection of doll clothes. Invite children to dress the bear for the weather. You may also purchase a large, durable paper bear that comes with four sets of clothes and accessories. Children can dress this weather bear for rainy, cool, hot, or cold weather. To order, call Carson-Dellosa Publishing; (800) 321-0943.

SCIENCE/LANGUAGE

Fluffy Cloud Walk

Students observe cumulus clouds and imagine the clouds are objects in the sky.

Materials

◎ old file folders cut in half at the fold

◎ scissors

◎ crayons or colored pencils

◎ cloud poster (bound into book)

◎ clipboard

◎ white construction paper, cut in the shape of a cloud

◎ journal pages (see page 8)

CAUTION: *Before going outside on any of your weather walks, remind children to protect their eyes by not looking directly into the sun.*

Teaching the Lesson

1 Pass out half of a file folder to every child. Demonstrate how to fold it in half and cut a window. (See illustration.) Have children think about clouds and then color pictures of all different sorts of clouds around the edges of their

windows. Their cloud catchers are ready!

2 Plan a weather walk on a day when the sky is filled with white, fluffy clouds. Use the poster to introduce children to this cloud type first. When you're ready to go, have children bring their cloud catchers. Take along the poster, a clipboard, pencils, and journal pages too.

3 Sit on the grass and invite children to suggest words that describe the clouds. Record each idea on the clipboard.

4 Ask children to "catch" special clouds inside their frames. As children look through their cloud catchers, discuss how the clouds move and change. Ask: What object does your cloud resemble? Show children the cloud poster and identify the shapes of the cloud pictures. Encourage children to find clouds in the sky that resemble animals, food, people, or other shapes.

SCIENCE NOTES

As children observe clouds they will notice clouds come in many different sizes, shapes, and colors. Cumulus clouds are big, fluffy, and white. They consist of billions of tiny water droplets. These droplets scatter the sunlight, causing the cloud to appear white. When cloud droplets collide, larger drops are formed. A cloud that consists of larger droplets can block the sunlight, causing the cloud to appear gray. Stratus clouds and cumulonimbus, or thunderclouds, are examples of gray clouds.

5 Pass out journal pages. Invite children to draw pictures of some of the cloud shapes they see.

6 Back in the classroom, involve the students as you transfer the descriptive words you recorded on the clipboard to the white construction-paper cloud. Display the cloud at the learning center (or mount on oak tag and hang from the ceiling).

JOURNAL Junctures Compare the clouds children sketched outdoors to the clouds they drew on their cloud catchers. Ask: How did your drawings improve after you studied the clouds?

ACTIVITY Extension This rhyme can be a finger-play or a flannel board subtraction activity.

Five white clouds went out to play
   (hold up five fingers)

Dancing in the sky one day
   (five fingers dance)

Wind came out and began to blow

Oooooo. . . Oooooo. . .

(blow on fingers)

One little cloud said, "Here I go!"
   (take away one finger)

Four white clouds went out to play, etc.

Three white clouds went out to play, etc.

Two white clouds went out to play, etc.

One white cloud went out to play, etc.

Literature Connection *It Looked Like Spilt Milk* by Charles G. Shaw (HarperCollins, 1947) is a patterned and predictable book that has everyone guessing about the white shapes that drift across each page. Write your own class book that uses the pattern: *Sometimes it looked like_____. But it wasn't _____.* Write out the phrase on a piece of light blue construction paper for each child. Help children complete the sentences with their own ideas about what a cloud may look like. Pass out white finger paint and have children illustrate their sentences with white, fluffy finger-painted clouds. When dry, put pages together to make a book. Don't forget to include the last page: *Sometimes it looked like spilt milk. But it wasn't spilt milk. But it was just a cloud in the sky.* Children will enjoy borrowing the book to share with their families.

Gray Cloud Walk

Students study rain clouds and make a weather forecast.

Materials

- cloud poster (bound into book)
- clipboard
- pencil
- markers
- gray construction paper (cut into cloud shape)
- voting graph, as shown, right

Teaching the Lesson

1. Plan a weather walk for a day the sky is filling with dark clouds. Use the poster to introduce this cloud type to children first. Before you go outside, be certain there is no lightning or thunder. Take along a clipboard and pencil.

2. Sit on the grass and encourage children to call out words that describe the dark clouds. Record their ideas on the clipboard.

3. Discuss the appearance of the sky before a rainstorm. Ask: Do you think it will rain today?

4. Back in the classroom record students' cloud words from the clipboard on the gray construction-paper cloud.

5. Display the gray cloud. If you've already taken a Fluffy Cloud Walk, place the gray cloud near the fluffy cloud. Compare the adjectives used to describe each cloud.

6. To wrap up the lesson, prepare and display the graph. (See right.) Have each child predict the weather by placing a marker on the graph. Watch the weather for the remainder of the day to confirm or disprove the predictions.

Wondering About Clouds?

Turn to page 34 and try the series of activities designed to explain how water moves upward to form clouds.

JOURNAL Junctures After the cloud walk, use the journal pages as an evaluation tool. Ask children to fold their pages in half. On one side ask them to draw the sky as it might look just before rain. On the other side have them draw the sky as it might look on a day that has no rain.

Literature Connection While sitting outside, read *Little Cloud* by Eric Carle (Philomel, 1996). Children may enjoy looking for their own "little cloud" up in the sky. Point out that at the end of the book, all of the clouds drift together, form one big cloud, and rain. Ask: Do you see that happening in the sky today?

ACTIVITY Extension Here's a song to go with your cloud-watching. Sing it again and again, so that every child has a chance to fill in the blank with a cloud shape. (Sing to the tune of "Ba Ba Black Sheep.")

Little cloud, little cloud
What are you today?

I am a _____

In the sky far away.

Learning Center Link

Post the Will It Rain Today? graph in the learning center. For the next week, ask children to observe the sky each morning on their way to school. As they gather in the morning, have each child place a marker on the graph to predict the weather that day. Just before dismissal, compare the graph to the actual weather conditions. Help children make the connection between cloud types and precipitation. The Cloud Book by Tomie de Paola (Holiday House, 1975) gives more information about predicting the weather with clouds.

READING/MOVEMENT

Wind Walk

Select a gusty day and look for signs of the wind.

Materials

◎ "Who Has Seen the Wind?" (see page 30)

◎ jar of bubbles, bubble wand

◎ balloons

◎ crepe-paper streamers or scarves

◎ trash bags

◎ pinwheel pattern (see page 31)

Teaching the Lesson

1. Begin by reading aloud the poem "Who Has Seen the Wind?" by Christina Rossetti. Ask: What happened when the wind was passing through?

2. Look out a window or sit in a sheltered area outside. Ask: Can you see the wind? Encourage children to explain how they know the wind is there.

3. Ask: Which direction is the wind blowing? Is it difficult to tell?

4. Once outside, lead the class in these activities.

◎ Run with the wind.

◎ Run into the wind. Which is easier?

◎ Run faster than the wind. Slower.

◎ Skip with the wind. Jump. Hop.

◎ Stand still and move your arms like the wind.

◎ Twirl and whirl like the wind.

◎ Wet a finger and hold it up in the air. What do you feel? (The wind will cool one side as it passes by.)

5. Provide streamers to run with and balloons to chase. Blow bubbles. Which way do they go? (Use the bags to collect balloons before going back inside.)

Literature Connection In *The Wind Garden* by Angela McAllister (Lothrop, Lee & Shepard, 1994), Ellie and her Grandpa "plant" a unique wind garden. Make pinwheels to plant using the pattern on page 31. Here's how:

◎ Have students cut out the square, color both sides, and cut on the dashed line. Be sure students don't go beyond the dashed lines. They need to stop cutting before the center dot.

- Show children how to take the point of each section and bend it over so that it touches the circle. Glue in place.

- Carefully stick a thumbtack through the center of each child's pinwheel into the eraser of an unsharpened pencil. Be sure the thumbtack is attached firmly while still allowing the pinwheel to spin.

- Let children "plant" their pinwheels in a flower bed or sandbox to create a wind garden then "pick" the pinwheels at the end of the day and take them home.

Learning Center Link

Make a recording of the poem "Who Has Seen the Wind?" and place it at the center along with a printed copy. Students can read along as they listen. Interested children can memorize the poem and recite it for the class. Others can add their own "signs of the wind" to create additional verses.

Wondering About Wind?

For more about wind, page 41 features a simple demonstration designed to explain that wind is moving air.

SCIENCE/LANGUAGE ARTS

Rainy Day Walk

Take advantage of a gentle rain to explore water flow, puddles, and the sound of rain.

Materials

- sentence strips
- rain gear
- foil pie plates
- foam meat trays
- light blue and dark gray construction paper, string

Teaching the Lesson

1. Begin this weather walk with a group meeting. Explain: Today we are going to be detectives. Invite children to offer definitions of the word *detective*, such as, a detective is someone who looks for clues in order to answer questions.

2. Use sentence strips to record these questions. Help the class read each one:

- Where is the biggest puddle on our playground and why is it so large?
- What do raindrops do when they land on the sidewalk?
- What do raindrops do when they land in the grass?
- What do raindrops do when they land on our raincoats?
- Do we have gutters on our school? How do gutters help with rain?

Divide the class into small groups and give each group one question to explore and then report about.

3. Before heading outside, model a sample investigation inside. If you have a window, make a sentence strip that reads: What do raindrops do when they land on a window? Post above the window, and gather students around. Model how to stop, observe, think, discuss, and report. For example, say: Let's look at the raindrops on the window. What are the raindrops doing? What happens when they run into each other? Explain that groups can follow the same procedure to explore their questions.

4 Dress for the rain and then walk around the school grounds looking for clues that will help answer each question.

5 Back inside, let each group of detectives share their findings.

ACTIVITY Extension Gather a collection of foil pie plates. Have children hold the pans over their heads and listen to the sounds the rain makes. Back in the classroom, demonstrate how to tap on the back of a foil pie pan with a pencil to make a raindrop sound. Introduce rain vocabulary by tapping out the speed and intensity of each type of rain on the tin. Let children tap out a drizzle, a sprinkle, a downpour, a steady rain, a light rain. What would "raining cats and dogs" sound like?

JOURNAL Junctures Return to the same area after the rain has stopped and the sun has dried the earth. Invite children to write or draw on journal pages to show what they think happened to the rain that was on the grass. Compare children's ideas about evaporation now and then again at the end of the unit.

Literature Connection Enrich your rainy day walk with these books.

Where Do Puddles Go? by Fay Robinson (Children's Press, 1995). A Rookie Read-About-Science book, this explains the water cycle in simple terms.

All Wet! All Wet! by James Skofield (HarperCollins, 1984). Join a young boy on his rainy day walk through a meadow.

Wondering About Clouds?

For hands-on activities that explain rain, turn to page 37: Why Do Clouds Drop Their Water?

Learning Center Link

Provide templates for raindrops. Let children use the patterns to cut raindrops out of blue construction paper. Have them write words that describe rain on both sides of their drops. Show children how to punch a hole in the top of each raindrop and tie on a string (precut to varying lengths). Provide sets of large cloud shapes cut from gray or black butcher paper. Have children tape the ends of their strings to one side of a cloud in each set, making sure the raindrops dangle beneath the cloud. Staple the sets of clouds together (strings inside) leaving a hole at the top. Stuff the clouds with newspaper to create a puffy rain cloud then staple to close. Punch a hole in the top of the clouds and sprinkle the rain clouds around the room.

Snow Walk

This activity has adaptations for those who live in warm climates so that all students can use their five senses to write snow poems.

SCIENCE NOTES

Are snow and crushed ice the same? While it is true that both snow and ice are frozen water, the frozen crystals in snow are interspersed with more air then are the frozen crystals in ice. That is why one cup of snow melts faster than one cup of ice and results in less water.

Materials

- ◎ snow or crushed ice
- ◎ resealable plastic bag
- ◎ brown paper lunch bag
- ◎ clipboard
- ◎ chart paper

Preparation

Out of sight of the children, fill the plastic bag with snow (or crushed ice). Seal the bag and put it inside the brown paper bag.

Teaching the Lesson

1 Show the bag to the children and ask them to predict its contents. Establish that this is difficult to do because they can not see, feel, smell, touch, or taste its contents!

2 Allow volunteers to gradually gather information using their five senses. First, have a volunteer hold the top of the bag to feel the weight of the contents. Next, have another child feel the bottom of the bag to explore the form. Then, demonstrate how to stick your nose inside the gathered top to smell without looking. Let several children reach inside the plastic bag in order to feel the snow. No peeking! After each observation, discuss which one of the five senses students are using to gather information. Finally, pull out the snow for all to see.

3 List each of the five senses on chart paper. Give each child a tiny bit of snow or crushed ice to hold. Ask: How does snow look, taste, smell, etc. Record students' words on the chart paper. If you've got snow in your area, take the class outside to expand on the list. Bring along a clipboard to record new words. Add them to the chart.

4 Have students use their ideas to write poems about snow. Here's one format they can follow.

Snow

   white (a sight word)

   cold (a touch word)

   crunchy (a sound word)

   clean (a smell word)

   frosty (a taste word)

Snow

ACTIVITY Extension  Use the class-created poetry to make a bulletin board. Ask several children to copy the

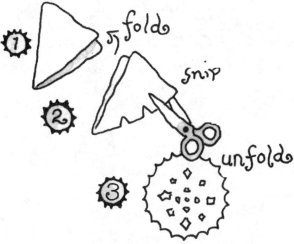

poems onto nice paper. Display the poems on the bulletin board. Other children can make coffee-filter snowflakes to sprinkle around the poems. (Demonstrate how to fold a coffee filter in half three times then snip around the edges with scissors. Open it up to reveal a unique snowflake design.)

Literature Connection Robert Frost's classic poem is brought to life by soft, wintry drawings in *Stopping by Woods on a Snowy Evening* (E.P. Dutton, 1978). Read the poem once without showing the pictures. Ask children to close their eyes and paint snowy pictures in their minds as they listen. Read the poem again and show the pictures. Talk about how illustrator Susan Jeffers interpreted the poem. Ask: What were you picturing? Check out what other poets are writing about the snow in *It's Snowing! It's Snowing!* by Jack Prelutsky (Greenwillow Books, 1984), a collection of more than a dozen fun-to-read poems.

Wondering About Clouds?

Why do some clouds make rain while others make snow? The activities on page 39 explain how temperature influences precipitation.

Learning Center Link

First thing in the morning, bring a bucket of snow inside the classroom. Set it on a plastic tablecloth in the learning center or place it in a sand table. Provide magnifying glasses, spoons, sand shovels, and other tools. Let children visit the snow in their free time. Have them draw pictures that illustrate how the snow looks now and how they believe the snow will look at lunch time, at the end of the day, and the next morning. Make observations at regular intervals. How is the snow changing? Why? Make one final observation the following morning.

Note: If you live in a warm climate, help children understand why it doesn't snow where they live by showing them the "snow point" on a thermometer, 32° F (0°C). Set the thermometer outside for several days and let children discover that it is not cold enough for snow. Soften their disappointment by substituting a bucket of crushed ice at the learning center.

Hot Weather Walk

Pair your little ones with older students for a scavenger hunt that teaches how the environment responds to heat.

Materials

◎ Sizzling Scavenger Hunt (see page 32)

◎ spritz-top water bottle

◎ paper cups

◎ container of cool water

For each group:

◎ clipboard

◎ yellow crayons

◎ plastic thermometer

◎ pencil

Preparation

On a hot, sunny day, invite students from an upper grade to act as guides for a sizzling scavenger hunt. Divide the class into small groups. Provide each with a set of materials. Set up a cool spot underneath a shade tree where children can gather to get a drink and a spray on the arm from the spritz bottle.

1. To begin, have the older students read one item at a time from the list, discuss it with the group, then step back as the younger children search.

2. When an item is found, have students record the information requested.

3. Wrap up by gathering everyone together in the cool spot to share and discuss findings.

 ACTIVITY Extension Brighten your room with these shiny suns!

◎ Make shiny yellow paint by mixing 1 cup corn syrup with about 20 drops yellow food coloring.

◎ Trace a large, simple sun shape on white construction paper (one per child).

◎ After the sun walk, have each child make a dark pencil drawing of a favorite summertime activity on the sun picture then cut it out. Help children add sentences that explain their drawings.

◎ Have children paint over their drawings and words with the transparent paint. Let dry for a day or two. Then brighten the hallway outside your room with the sunny art.

Literature Connection *Sun Song* by Jean Marzollo (HarperCollins, 1995) is a beautifully illustrated book that describes the sun's activities from sunrise to sunset in a country setting. After sharing the book, have children recall each of the sun's activities as you list them on chart paper. For example:

◎ call the sheep

◎ kiss the face of a child

◎ touch the feathers of a bird

Follow up by brainstorming a list of verbs that describe the sun's actions the children observed on the sun walk. For example:

◎ warmed the sidewalk

◎ dried up a puddle

◎ touched my arms and face

◎ cast a shadow

Children might like to illustrate their ideas for a class book about the sun's activities.

Who Has Seen the Wind?

by Christina Rossetti

Who has seen the wind?

Neither I nor you:

But when the leaves hang trembling,

The wind is passing through.

Who has seen the wind?

Neither you nor I:

But when the trees bow down their heads,

The wind is passing by.

Pinwheel Pattern

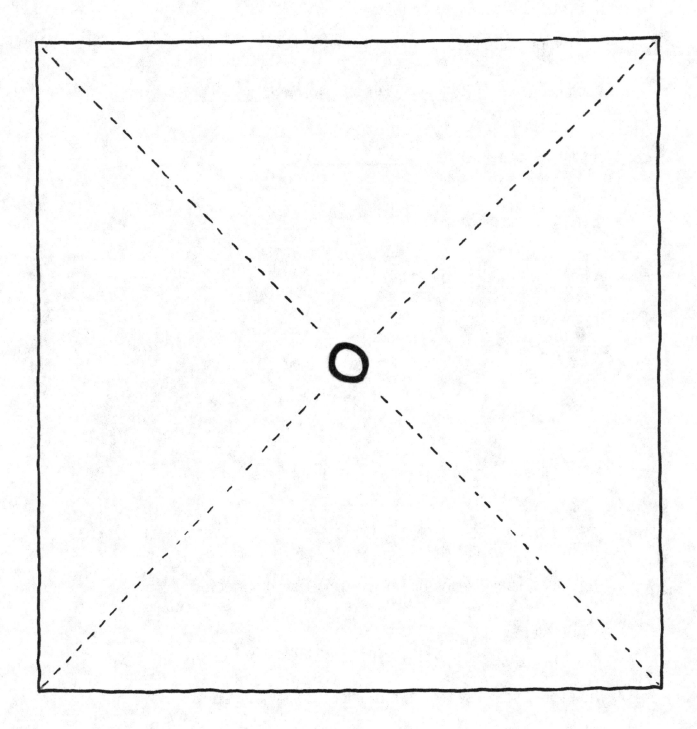

Sizzling Scavenger Hunt

1. The temperature today:

Our estimate _____ Our measurement _____

2. A sunny spot (tell where): _____

3. A shady spot (tell where): _____

4. A tree shadow (draw a picture):

5. A plant that is bending toward the sun (tell where):

_____

6. The hottest spot (use the thermometer to test your idea):

Temperature _____ Place _____

7. The coolest spot (use the thermometer to test your idea):

Temperature _____ Place _____

Wondering About Weather

What are clouds made of? What makes the wind blow? Children are full of questions like these—questions that are sometimes difficult to answer! This section contains simple activities that will help children deepen their understanding of basic weather concepts. Instead of teaching this section in isolation, you can weave these activities into your weather unit as the questions naturally emerge.

QUESTION 1

What Are Clouds Made Of?

SCIENCE NOTES

A cloud is a large collection of very tiny droplets of water or ice crystals. The droplets are so small and light they can float in the air. All air contains water, but near the ground it is usually in the form of an invisible gas called water vapor. When warm air rises, it expands and cools. Cool air cannot hold as much water vapor as warm air, so some of the vapor condenses onto tiny pieces of dust that are floating in the air and forms a tiny droplet around each dust particle. When billions of these droplets come together they become a visible cloud. In this activity, children see clouds form when they breath on spoons. When warm, moist breath hits the cool spoon, water vapor condenses and turns into a cloud—or water you can see.

PART 1: Make a Cloud

Students discover that clouds are made of water droplets.

Materials

◎ a can of shaving cream

◎ 1 metal spoon per child

Teaching the Lesson

1 Ask: What if clouds were made of shaving cream? Squirt a dollop of shaving cream onto each child's work space. Identify the shaving cream as clouds: That one is fluffy like a cumulus cloud. Can you make it wispy like a cirrus cloud or low and layered like a stratus cloud? Remind students to look at the cloud poster as they work.

2 Pass out wet paper towels and have everyone remove the shaving cream. The tables will be squeaky clean!

3 Continue the lesson: We know that clouds are not made of shaving cream, but what are clouds made of? Have children share their ideas.

4 Have children cup their hands around their mouths and exhale into their hands. Repeat several times. Help children to notice that their breath feels warm and moist.

5 Pass out the spoons. Have children notice that the spoons feel cool. Hold the back of a spoon close to your mouth and exhale. Have the children repeat this procedure. What do they see? (A tiny cloud will appear.) Help children understand that the tiny clouds on their spoons are like the clouds in the sky, formed when warm, moist air and cool air come together.

ACTIVITY Extension There is water in the air! Mix up a batch of icy lemonade in a glass pitcher. Before you serve it, set out the pitcher for all to see. Watch as water starts to drip down the sides of the pitcher. Challenge children to explain where the water came from. (When warm air comes in contact with the icy cold pitcher, water vapor condenses on the pitcher.) **NOTE:** *This demonstration works best on a warm, humid day.*

If your class enjoyed the shaving cream clouds they will also enjoy *Cloudy with a Chance of Meatballs* by Judith Barrett (Macmillan, 1982). This story takes place in the town of Chewandswallow where it rains soup and snows mashed potatoes!

PART 2: Introducing a Droplet

This lesson helps children to visualize the many droplets that are in a cloud and also provides practice with estimating and counting by tens.

Materials

- ◎ One Drop (see page 42)
- ◎ overhead transparency
- ◎ overhead marker
- ◎ overhead projector
- ◎ a cup of blue-tinted water
- ◎ an eyedropper

Preparation

Make a class set of the One Drop reproducible. Make a copy on an overhead transparency too.

Teaching the Lesson

1 Use an eyedropper to place a drop of blue water on the screen of an overhead projector. Explain: This drop of water may seem small but it is huge compared to a cloud droplet. Clouds are made of droplets. A drop of water this size may contain as many as a million cloud droplets! While comprehending *one million* may be too abstract for young children, they love to consider big numbers and will have fun visualizing and discussing the many droplets in a raindrop. (See Literature Connection, page 36, to explore the concept of one million in greater depth.)

2 Dry off the projector screen and project the overhead transparency copy of One Drop. Explain that the tiny dots represent cloud droplets. Ask: How many droplets do you think are in this drop? Demonstrate how you might estimate a large number by eyeballing groups of 10. (Do not reveal the total. There are 100 droplets.)

3 To help students get an idea of how big the number one million is, pass out a copy of One Drop to each child. Have children follow the directions to complete the page. Compare the numbers 100 and 1,000,000. Which is bigger?

4 Invite children to add more droplets to their drop to try to make one million. As they work, they'll probably stop often to ask "Is this a million?" Eventually, they'll get the idea that one million is a really big number—more than they can draw!

5 Have children cut out their drops, cluster together, and hold their drops above their heads to form a "cloud."

Invite children to use their experience clustering together like a cloud (see step 5, above) to write about how it might feel to be a cloud droplet.

Cover a bulletin board with blue paper. Add a title: *Clouds are made of water droplets.* Use white chalk or a white crayon to draw a cloud outline on the blue paper. Fill in the outline with the drops from the activity. Children who are interested will enjoy making additional drops for the display.

Learning Center Link

Make a sign for the learning center that says: There can be 1,000,000 droplets of water in one drop of water. Place a calculator in the center and have children practice punching in the number 1,000,000. Add an estimating jar filled with a small number of buttons (or beans, pennies, and so on). Have children write their names and estimates on paper and drop them into a box or envelope. At the end of the week have children count the objects and compare their estimates. Increase the items in the estimating jar each week.

Literature Connection How Much Is a Million by David M. Schwartz (Lothrop, Lee & Shepard, 1985) will help children make sense of big numbers. After you read this book, place it in the learning center next to the estimating jar.

SCIENCE

QUESTION 2

How Does Water Get Up to the Clouds?

SCIENCE NOTES

When children see puddles disappear after a rain they assume that the water no longer exists. As adults we can understand that the puddle has evaporated and turned into vapor, a state that cannot be perceived with the five senses. Over time, and as they progress developmentally, children will also understand these facts. For now, use the following activities to emphasize the tangible. In each, children observe drops of water rather than larger amounts to reinforce the concept that clouds are made up of droplets. Evaporation and freezing also take less time to occur with the drops, enabling young children to more easily understand the science.

Adopt a Drop

Students will observe one drop of water evaporating and speculate about where it has gone.

Materials

- Blast Off! (see page 43)
- laminating film, clear contact paper, or snack-size reclosable bags
- eyedropper
- cup of water

Preparation

Duplicate page 43 for each child. Laminate each copy or cover with contact paper. Cut the page into three parts, as indicated. Save the lower two sections for later activities. (As an alternative to laminating, you can seal

Blast Off! inside snack-size reclosable bags. Trim the sides for a snug fit inside the bags.) Plan to start this activity at least two hours before children leave school for the day to allow them time to make beginning and ending observations.

Teaching the Lesson

1. Ask: If clouds are made of droplets of water how does the water get up to the clouds?

2. Give each child a water-resistant copy of Blast Off! Have the children place their pages somewhere in the room where they will not be disturbed.

3. Circulate around the room and use the eyedropper to place one drop of water in the circle on the Blast Off! page.

4. Recite 10, 9, 8, 7, 6 . . . as children observe their drops. Did anything happen? Explain that it takes time for the water to "blast off" to the clouds.

5. Check the drops at regular intervals. Depending on the temperature of the room and the humidity, it will take about two hours for the drop to disappear. Did the drop disappear all at one time? (no, a little at a time)

ACTIVITY Extension Demonstrate that heat speeds up the evaporation process. Preheat an electric skillet and gather children around. Keep everyone at a safe distance. Explain that you are about to use an eyedropper to put several drops of water on the hot surface of the skillet. Have children predict what will happen. How will it be different than setting a drop out in the classroom as before? Drop the water into the skillet and watch as it dances and then disappears. Explain: The heat of the skillet moves the water up into the air very quickly. What is the heat source that caused the drop in the room to disappear? (for example, room temperature) What is the heat source that causes a puddle on the playground to disappear? (the sun)

Literature Connection Read *Where Do Puddles Go?* by Fay Robinson (Children's Press, 1995) to help children understand how the water, sun, and clouds are connected. Then go outside and look for places from which the clouds may "gather" water droplets. Could water be moving up from a puddle children spot? The drinking fountain? The trees and grass? To capture water on its way to the clouds, turn a clear plastic tumbler upside down in a sunny spot on the grass. After a few minutes water droplets will appear on the inside of the glass. Eventually the droplets will fall back into the grass to create a mini water cycle under the glass.

SCIENCE

QUESTION 3

Why Do Clouds Drop Water?

 **SCIENCE NOTES**

Not all clouds produce rain. Clouds continually evaporate and replenish themselves. But when the conditions are right and a cloud loses sufficient heat, its droplets cluster together and form larger drops. The drops are too heavy to float on the air currents and they succumb to the pull of gravity and fall to the earth. In this way, water moves continuously from ocean, to air, to land, and back to the ocean again. This is the water cycle.

Drops Get Together

Students explore the principle of cohesion as they push drops of water together to make a rain cloud that can really rain.

Materials

- ◎ Drops Get Together (see the middle section of page 43)
- ◎ toothpicks
- ◎ eyedroppers
- ◎ cup of water, tinted blue

Preparation

For this activity you will need the middle section of page 43. Save the lower section for another activity. If you did not laminate these pages (or cover with contact paper), place Drops Get Together inside snack-size reclosable bags. Trim the sides for a snug fit inside the bags. This activity works best in small teacher-directed groups.

Teaching the Lesson

1. Gather a small group of children around a table to review some of the concepts they have learned in the weather unit. Ask: What are clouds made of? How does water get up to the clouds? Do all clouds rain or snow? Can it rain if there are no clouds in the sky?

2. Explain that today children will see what happens inside of a cloud. Pass out a water-resistant copy of Drops Get Together to each child.

3. Help the children use an eyedropper to place one drop of water in each circle under the cloud. Explain: These three drops represent the tiny bits of water that blasted off from your water drop. (See Blast Off!, page 36.) They are also like the tiny bits of water that are continually leaving ponds,

puddles, plants, and the ocean. As tiny bits of our drops of water blasted off from our classroom, they moved slowly upward toward the clouds.

Note: *Emphasize that real water bits are so small they cannot be seen by the human eye. The water drops children are using simply represent water bits.*

4. Have each child use a toothpick to manipulate the drops until they are inside of the cloud.

5. Say: Clouds can be very cold. Once the droplets are inside of a cloud they huddle together. Have the children push the three drops together. What happened when the three droplets touched each other? (They became one drop.)

6. Say: Now they are no longer droplets, they are drops. Droplets are light and can float in the air but drops are too heavy to float. Can you guess what happens to a drop that is too heavy to float in the air? Have children tip the paper and cause the drop to fall out of the cloud. It's raining!

Literature Connection Students can use page 43 to make their own water-cycle booklets to read and share with their families. First have them cut out the pages and color. For fun, children might like to add sea creatures or boats. Punch a hole in the upper left corner of each page. Bind the pages with a tiny O-ring. Just like the water-cycle, this book has no beginning and no end, it just keeps circling around again and again!

Learning Center Link

Set up a water cycle for your learning center. You will need a clear plastic shoe box, a small bowl of water, a flexible-neck lamp, and a reclosable plastic bag full of ice.

◎ *Place the bowl of water inside the box at one end and close the lid. Position the lamp so that it shines on the water.*

◎ *Tell children that the water is like a puddle and the lamp is like the sun. Have them draw what they believe will happen on their journal pages. (See page 8.)*

◎ *After about two hours have children stop back at the center, remove the lid, and draw another picture of what actually happened.*

◎ *Replace the lid and place a bag of ice on the end, opposite the bowl of water. Remind children that high in the sky the air is cool. Again, have children draw what they believe will happen.*

◎ *After about two hours have children remove the ice and the lid and check the box. What made it "rain" inside of the box? (The heat from the lamp causes the water in the bowl to evaporate. When the water vapor comes in contact with the cooler surface at the top of the box, it condenses. Droplets of water collect on the inside of the lid. After a while, the drops come together and fall like rain.)*

Place ice on lid here.

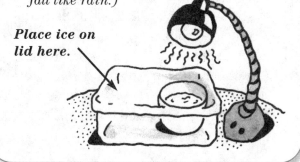

QUESTION 4

Why Do Some Clouds Make Rain and Some Make Snow?

SCIENCE NOTES

If the temperature of the air in a cloud is below the freezing point, snow crystals may grow directly from the water vapor. Sometimes snowflakes melt before they reach the ground and what started out as snow reaches the earth as rain. Sleet forms if the air between the cloud and the earth is below freezing. Sleet starts out as rain but freezes on the way down. Whatever the combination, air temperature determines what will form in a cloud and fall to the ground.

Cool Off

Students will continue to observe the behavior of a drop of water. This time their drops will spend some time in freezing temperatures.

Materials

◎ Cool Off (see page 43)

- eyedropper
- cup of water, tinted blue
- cookie sheet or tray

Preparation

You will need the last section of page 43 for this activity. If you did not laminate these pages (or cover with contact paper), place Cool Off inside snack-size reclosable bags. Trim the sides for a snug fit.

Teaching the Lesson

1 Why do some clouds produce rain while others produce snow? Let children share their ideas then give each child a copy of Cool Off As a review, remind children of the activities they have done with a drop of water (watched it evaporate, simulated rain).

2 Give each child one drop of water inside the circle on Cool Off. Ask: What do you think will happen if the temperature surrounding the drop were to get very cold?

3 Transfer Cool Off papers and drops to a cookie sheet or tray. If your outside temperature is below 32°F (0°C), place the tray outside. Otherwise, use a freezer.

4 Wait one hour. Have children pick up their papers and drops. Ask: How did the cold air change your drop?

JOURNAL Junctures After discussing the question in step four, pass out journal pages. (See page 8.) Have students draw pictures to show how they think cold air changes droplets of water that are in clouds.

Learning Center Link

Photographs in Snowballs *by Lois Ehlert (Harcourt, Brace, Jovanovich, 1995) will inspire children to create their own snow people and snow animal collages. The last few pages of the book will enhance their understanding of the states of water too. After reading the book, stock the center with small, medium, and large white construction paper circles, buttons, glue, scissors, colored construction paper, and other supplies. Children can use the materials to make their own snow figures.*

SCIENCE

QUESTION 5

What Is Wind?

SCIENCE NOTES

What is wind? Wind is moving air. It is common for children to believe that wind causes air to move. However, wind is not the force that drives the air—the sun is. Wind results because the sun heats the earth unevenly. Air above hot areas of the earth expands and rises. Cooler, denser air rushes in to replace the heated air. Wind is the movement of air from a high pressure area to a low pressure area.

Capture the Wind

Students will capture a bag of wind and discover that what they have is a bag of air.

Materials

◎ clear plastic bags

◎ a breezy day

JOURNAL Junctures Prior to this investigation, ask children: What do you know about the wind? Have them record ideas on journal pages.

Teaching the Lesson

1. Make a wind word web. Have children share ideas and questions from their journal pages.

2. Give each child a clear plastic bag. Go outside to capture wind: Wave an open bag in the air until it is inflated. Twist the opening to capture the air inside of the bag.

3. Have everyone bring their wind bags back inside, holding the tops securely closed. Take time to observe the bags of wind. Record additional ideas on the wind web.

4. Ask: Do you think you have wind in your bag or do you think you have air? This question will be confusing but it will initiate an interesting conversation.

5. Explain that once they caught the air and contained it in the bag it ceased to be wind. In order for air to be wind it must be on the move.

6. Close the lesson with a bang! While still pinching the opening of the bags, allow children to bang the bottoms of their bags and send the wind on its way again.

ACTIVITY Extension What makes the wind blow? Try this to demonstrate the answer. You will need:

◎ an empty soda bottle

◎ a balloon

◎ a thermos full of hot water

Place the balloon over the mouth of the bottle. Pour a few inches of hot water into a cup. Set the soda bottle in the hot water. After a few moments, the balloon will stand straight up as the air inside the bottle warms and expands into the balloon. Explain that as the sun warms air around the earth, the air rises. Colder air then moves in to fill the vacant spot. What is moving air called? Wind!

Literature Connection If this activity stirs up more questions than it answers, share these books, which explain the science behind wind.

Feel the Wind by Arthur Dorros (Crowell, 1989). This book explores the cause and effect of wind.

I Wonder Why the Wind Blows and Other Questions About Our Planet by Anita Ganeri (Kingfisher, 1994). This book answers common questions children have about weather.

Learning Center Link

Search for pictures in magazines that show increasing wind speeds. For example, you may have a picture of a family picnic in a light breeze, a picture of a girl flying a kite, a picture of the ocean with waves pounding the shore, and a picture of a tornado or hurricane. Have children place the pictures in order of wind strength, from a light breeze to tornado winds.

Name_____

One Drop

1. How many droplets are inside of this drop?

My estimate _____

2. Circle groups of 10 droplets. Count by tens.

There are _____ groups of ten in this drop.

3. How many droplets are inside this drop?

My count _____

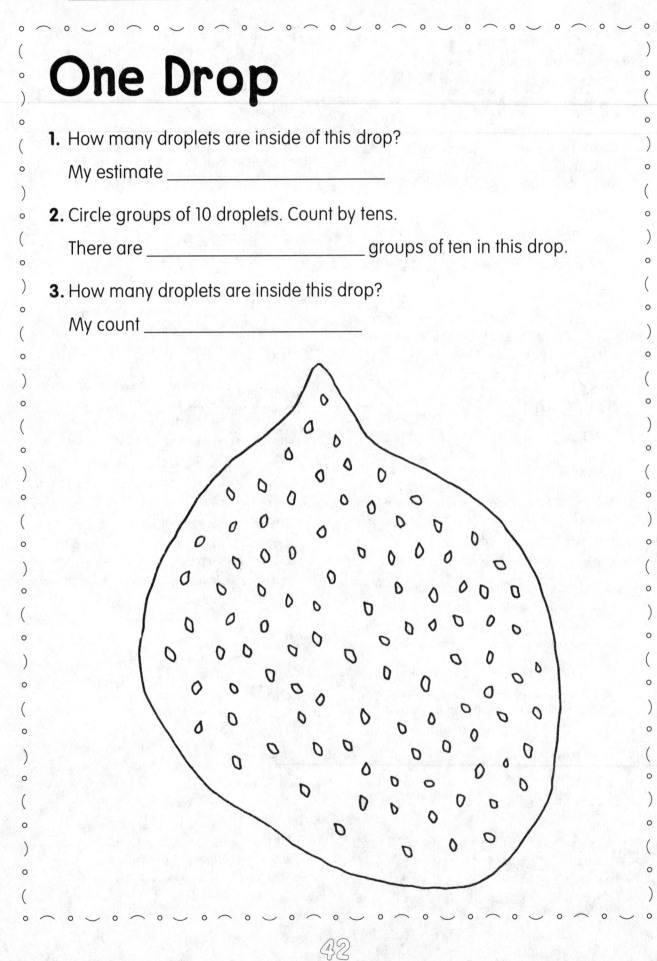

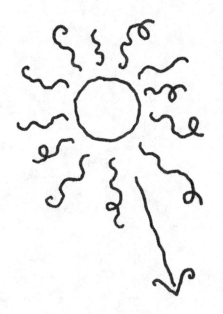

Sun warms the water.

Water rises.

Water gets together and
forms a cloud.

Water falls as rain.

Name_____

Blast Off!

Name_____

Drops Get
Together

Name_____

Cool Off

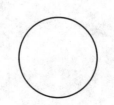

Celebrate Weather!

Celebrate your students' weather discoveries by planning a day of weather fun—complete with guests and activity stations. Following are suggestions for planning your special day.

Setting Up Your Celebration

For the young child, a celebration is a time to break from the daily routine and participate in something special. The ideas sprinkled on these pages will help you design an end-of-the-unit weather wrap-up that will celebrate students' learning accomplishments and encourage new skills in a creative context.

Browse through the ideas, set up your activity stations, and celebrate weather together.

Special Guests

In addition to inviting parents to be your guests at the celebration, ask a weather reporter to join you. Ask the speaker to share information about his or her job. Then let children demonstrate for the guest how they give the daily weather report at My First Weather Station. Suggest that the weather reporter bring a camera crew to tape the presentation in order to show a clip of the children's accomplishments on the evening weather report.

Activity Stations

Ask parents to rotate through these activity stations with their children. Post directions at each station for easy reference.

MOVE LIKE THE WEATHER

Set up a creative-movement center. Pass out paper streamers. Turn on some classical music for inspiration and present these movement opportunities.

Be a leaf: The wind has just blown you off a tree.

Be a snowflake: You are falling, twirling, fluttering to the ground.

Be a bolt of lightning: You are crashing from a cloud.

Be a raindrop: In a sprinkle; in a downpour.

Be a tornado: You are whirling and twirling!

WEATHER REPORTING

Set up a desk and chairs next to My First Weather Station. Provide dress clothes as props for children to dress up as anchors. Have them sit behind the desk and record a weather report (videotape, if possible). Children not engaged in other activities can watch and then take their turn.

SNOW CONES

Provide a bucket of crushed ice, a scoop, paper cups, spoons, and powdered juice mix. Have children scoop ice into cups, sprinkle with powder, and enjoy their snow cones!

CUMULOUS CLOUD SNACKS

Pop up a batch of cumulous clouds (popcorn) and let visitors help themselves to a handful. Display the cloud poster here (bound in the back of the book) and encourage parents and children to talk about the clouds they see outside. Are they white and fluffy like the popcorn? What kinds of shapes can they see? Provide file folders for making cloud catchers too. (See page 21.) What special cloud shapes can they "catch" in their frames? Finally, share a copy of *The Little Cloud*, by Eric Carle, for parents and children to read together.

WACKY SUNGLASSES

Provide pipe cleaners, six-pack rings cut in groups of two, and colored cellophane. Make a model by gluing cellophane over the rings and trimming to fit. Add pipe cleaners for side pieces and twist the ends to fit around each ear. Let children visit this station to make their own play sunglasses. Discuss how real sunglasses protect us from the sun.

MY FAVORITE WEATHER

Provide paper and paint. Fold back one inch at the bottom of the page. Ask children to paint a picture that shows their favorite type of weather. Unfold the paper to take dictation or have the child write a sentence at the bottom of the page.

WINDOW WEATHER

Make colorful weather symbols to decorate windows. You will need:

- ◎ sun, snowflake, and raindrop templates
- ◎ cardboard
- ◎ fabric paint in squeeze tubes
- ◎ glitter
- ◎ waxed paper

1 Tape each template to a small piece of cardboard to give it stability, then cover with waxed paper.

2 Have children trace a weather shape on the waxed paper with fabric paint (be certain that there are no broken lines in the paint), then sprinkle the design with glitter.

3 Set the waxed paper aside to allow the designs to dry. Place a new sheet of waxed paper over the templates for a new group of children. Designs will dry in about 48 hours. Just peel and stick to a window!